AF488923

DEDICATED TO

JACK BUTCHER, POW, FIGHTER PILOT

FLIGHT LEADER ON MEMORIAL DAY

REST IN PEACE JACK

High Flight

Oh! I have slipped the surly bonds of Earth

And danced the skies on laughter-silvered wings;

Sunward I've climbed, and joined the tumbling mirth

of sun-split clouds, - and done a hundred things

You have not dreamed of - wheeled and soared and swung,

high in the sunlit silence.   Hov'ring there,

I've chased the shouting wind along, and flung

my eager craft through footless halls of air....

Up, up the long, delirious, burning blue

I've topped the windswept heights with easy grace,

Where never lark, or even eagle flew -

And, while with silent lifting mind I've trod

The high untrespassed sanctity of space,

Put out my hand, and touched the face of God.

John Gillespie Magee Jr.

Prologue

Come with me on an adventure and a journey. Watch for amazing miracles along the way.

I once read that everyone has six moments in their life when they were close to death and, most of the time, did not even know it. Your adventure will begin as you join me in the cockpit of a Mach 2 fighter jet as we set off on some harrowing missions and count to six or more.

Your journey will take you from the deep poverty of the urban projects to a life of success and fulfillment.

I hope you enjoy it.

TABLE OF CONTENTS

Up From The Projects

Chapter 1 – Alert Barn Hustle

Just jogging around the alert barn. It takes a lot of laps to get in a couple of miles. But what else is there to do when you are sitting on alert for 48 hours at a time? The alert barn is a structure that resembles an aircraft hangar which houses two fully armed Mach 2 fighter jets, whose mission is to defend the coast of the United States. Between the two fighter enclosures is a fully equipped two story living quarters. The first floor is for the aircraft crew chiefs. They are responsible for maintaining and launching the fighter aircraft once the klaxon sounds. The second floor is the pilots' quarters.

During the cold war, a picket line of these barns spread across the borders of the US. Our target was the feared Russian Bear bomber or its cousin the Blinder, a supersonic Russian bomber. In reality, it was too far for those bombers to threaten the Pacific Northwest, so most of our missions were to redirect lost commercial aircraft or to respond to simulated intrusions to test our readiness.

It was for the most part a boring job. Just hurry up and wait. The time was our own as we waited and waited. But the excitement would start when the alert horn blasted, and the aircraft were "scrambled." We were required to have that fighter airborne in five minutes and on the way to its intended target.

So, I am jogging, trying to kill some time, and keep myself in shape on this sunny day at Kingsley Field, in the sleepy town of Klamath Falls, Oregon. It takes some preparation I might add. I hang my flight suit on the aircraft's ladder with the boots open and ready to don. But the chances of a scramble...not very high.

And then the klaxon blasts and things get exciting fast. I run for the aircraft, slip my flight suit over my sweaty body, and throw on the boots. My crew chief helps me into the cockpit and into my parachute. We crank up the engines. I look over and see my wingman, Tactical Call Sign "Buda," donning his helmet, and in seconds we are ready to roll, and we are off...almost anyway. It seems that Buda is having mechanical issues. He has blown a starter. It does not look like I will have a wingman today. I hit the runway in my single seat, single engine F-106, light the afterburner and am off, not knowing where or why.

I am airborne for a brief time and departure control hands me over to the Tactical Radar Controllers. They are the ones who point me to the target. They own me now. My mission is their mission, and I get the feeling that this is indeed one of those fake intrusions. Regardless, I have a job, and it is not going to be easy with my wingman sitting at home.

'Mayday, mayday, mayday!!!!' Aircraft down, aircraft down!!! Things take a sudden turn. Yes, it was an intrusion test, and I was not the first line of defense to be so tested. My fighter pilot friends from Comox, the Canadian Air Force Base on Vancouver Island, were scrambled to the same fake intruder. In this case it was an old B-57 bomber, an aircraft way past its prime and relegated to the mission of copying the tactics that a Russian bomber might employ.

The Canadians were flying an aircraft called the F-101 Voodoo. It was designed to intercept bombers just as my F-106 was, but it lacked maneuverability. It had a high tail and if it pulled too many G's, the tail would lose its airflow, and the plane would become uncontrollable and sometimes go into a spin from which it was unrecoverable. I remember visiting Comox one time just after a Canadian friend of mine pulled too many G's in the traffic pattern, lost control of the aircraft, and had to eject just off the shoreline. His F-101 gently drifted into the bay and the two of them were picked from the water without incident. When they pulled the 101 from the bay it was still remarkably intact.

The F-101 had passed the test as I was awaiting my turn. It is hard not to celebrate when the mission is accomplished and that is exactly what the F-101 pilot did.

He and his back seater successfully intercepted the B-57

and, according to the B-57 pilot, the F-101 pilot decided

to show off and pulled a hard ascending turn, a bit too

hard. The aircraft flipped into a spin and went down

about a hundred miles off the coast of Northern Oregon.

My mission had gone from routine to intense. Two souls

floated in the ocean, status unknown. Instead of a test

we were now in a rescue operation.

Chapter 2 – The Twersky Essay

It is a bitter, freezing winter day with wind blasting from Lake Erie. It is called the lake effect. It is a brutal four miles, and always a tough decision. Walk it or spend 15 cents to catch the bus home. It sounds like a ridiculously stupid decision, but in those days minimum wage was a dollar an hour and few people in the Projects had dollars to waste. So today it was a walk, and a day that molded me in a way I never expected.

It was the last mile to the Projects, walking down Perry Street, lightly dressed with that gusty wind blowing against my back and making me ask myself, "how will I make it...this last mile?" And then it hit me. "I am the Master of my fate, I am the Captain of my soul," from a poem by William Ernest Henley called <u>Invictus</u>. I determined at that point that I would not be defeated by the fierce winds of Lake Erie blowing through the streets of Buffalo, New York, or any other obstacles. It was a turning point. I never looked back.

The next day I trudged back to the Buffalo Science Center and continued my research. I am 13 years young and working on my entry for the Twersky Science Essay contest. It pits seventh grade writers in the city against one another. I write it and rewrite it in cursive. Typewriters were a luxury that the Project people didn't have. No problem, just write it again and again, in cursive.

It is awards night at the Buffalo Science Center. Mom and I were sitting in the front row of a large room of people. They are announcing the winners. They name the top five award winners in ascending order. Each marches to the stage. Each dressed to the hilt in expensive suits and shined shoes. It is time to name first place. The winner... from Public School No. 4... Bruce Miller!! The crowd applauded politely, and I walked to the stage. Suddenly the applause turned into laughter as this ragamuffin kid appeared, dressed in sneakers and a blue vest, and standing a foot shorter than the line of the four runners-up. I was proud, but also humiliated. But you know what? I won!

It was after the ceremony. The essays were displayed on stands around the room. "The Story of a Rotting Log" was the theme. As I walked around the room and looked at the other prize winners' essays, I noticed that they were all nicely typed and professional looking. Then I came to

my own essay pasted on the wall. It was in cursive...

It was a start!

Chapter 3 – Alert Barn Scramble – Part 2

We are 100 miles off the coast of Oregon, and I have been dramatically inserted into a rescue operation. Two Canadian F-101 crewmembers had lost control of their aircraft and were forced to eject.

The ejection was a success. The B-57 pilot saw a couple of chutes and circled them until they entered a dense cloud formation. He was running on fumes, so he had to make a quick exit after he focused my attention on where my two brethren had entered the "soup."

My job was to find and support the rescue operation in any way I could, and it was not going to be easy with the heavy clouds and precipitation. Down I ventured, lower and lower, constantly monitoring the altimeter (which measures my altitude). Finally at about 1,000 feet I picked up a few patches of open sky. One thousand feet was our minimum altitude those days, but it was clear that this day required an "out of the box solution."

It is not easy picking up a raft bobbing in the turbulent ocean, especially when you are traveling 300 knots at 500 feet above the ocean floor. The last thing you want to be is that third person floating in the ocean. I am in a constant 3-4 G turn and not having much luck as my eyes dart from the altimeter, trying to stay above the ocean floor, and searching for those tiny yellow rafts. The only thing I could see was a huge oil slick from where the F-101 had crashed into the ocean. Suddenly, I had an idea.

When the F-101 crashed into the ocean it created an oil slick, which now had spread out and almost looked like an arrow. I figured if I could use it as a marker and fly a series of patterns, I might get a glimpse of the two. You see, after the ejection the wind should have pushed the parachutes in a certain direction. If my thinking was correct, that same wind was pushing the oil slick and creating a pointer that should lead to the downed crew. I started my pattern, and after a couple of tries, I saw a yellow raft. It was too small to be able to recognize whether there was one or two, or whether a pilot was on board and healthy, but I had to assume that they were OK. I kept that pattern going repeatedly, constantly relying on the oil slick as my guide.

After what seemed like an eternity, a rescue C-130 Hercules arrived on scene. He had all the equipment to drop to the two downed airmen. My job, at this point, was to get the eyes of the C-130 pilot onto the bobbing rafts. After several failed attempts at oral direction, I decided to slip behind the C-130 and direct him from the rear. When we were just about over the rafts, I kicked the plane into afterburner and flew under the C-130 so that we would both fly over the rafts together. I was skimming the waves, but that is what it took. I heard a "Tally Ho" from the rescue crew, which means "eyes on the target" in aviation terms.

As I headed back to base, my job was done, except for one thing. I really could not tell if there were two live and healthy pilots on those rafts. My heart swelled for those guys. I began to pray. "Lord, I just pray your hand on those two airmen. That they be safe and able to return to their families." I prayed that prayer many times before I recovered my jet to Kingsley Field and did a few exhilarating high speed traffic patterns to celebrate my success.

My friends from Comox were plucked from the ocean by

a Coast Guard helicopter a couple of hours later. None

the worse for wear, but with an amazing adventure to

talk about at the bar that evening.

Chapter 4 – Grandma's House

In a child's mind every experience seems normal, even the most bizarre and repressive behaviors. We did not know how crazy Grandma was until a few years later. It is easy to understand where it came from. As a young laborer, Grandma's hand was crushed in an industrial accident. Her lifelong handicap kept her out of the workforce. I can never recall her having a career or even a job. She married at an early age, but, according to her conversations, it was not known to be a blissful union. Our mother was born in 1928, an only child. Frederick, our grandfather, died when the iron beams on the truck he was unloading broke from their cable packing and killed him instantly. Mother had just turned eight. Grandma heard the ambulances heading for the accident and found out later from the constable that Grandpa was gone.

I can only imagine how my mother's world changed at 8 years old. She was locked in the home for the most part and barely left. Mom never finished eighth grade. Grandma was a hermit, so company was rare. Little doubt then that the first man Mom met, my father, she married, at the early age of 17. It was partly because any life was better than Grandma's place. I hope that the marriage was a sometimes happy one. It was fruitful enough. Six kids born from 1946 to 1957.

Father was a military man: an airborne ranger and paratrooper. He just missed the Great War but distinguished himself in Vietnam as a member of the famous Army "Green Beret" fraternity. I still have his iconic symbol-the green beret-of that elite group in my stash of memorabilia.

In my father's first overseas deployment, when I was three or four years old, we ended up at our grandmother's house in Buffalo, New York. There were the four of us. Alice was the oldest, David Eugene (Gene) next, me being number three, and Dana, the baby, two years my junior. The rules were strict. The three eldest each had a corner in the kitchen, and we were expected to remain there all day. No wandering the house, no outside play, and toys were out of the question. Baby Dana was the favorite and had free reign of things. Day after day after day, in what seemed an eternity, the three of us elder children sat bored silly.

With nothing left to do, I picked up the only book in the house, a Bible. I started reading it. I read that book from the beginning to the end, including "A begat B and B begat C, etc, etc, etc." It was not a religious experience, but one born out of boredom. As it turned out, when I hit first grade, I could read at a fourth-grade level, amazing the teachers. That bizarre head start turned out to be somewhat of a blessing.

After my father's overseas tour ended, the family headed back to Fort Bragg, North Carolina. The family grew. Philip was the next child and Valerie brought up the rear.

Things were not happy on the home front. The family was fractured. My father preferred to spend his evenings at the club drinking. He became an alcoholic and would holler and beat us with the belt during his drunken spells. Not a pretty picture.

Meanwhile, I dazzled the teachers with my reading and math skills through grade three, when life took another turn.

Chapter 5 – Night Air-to-Air Refueling

Night air-to-air refueling is a challenging mission. Tonight, it presents an even more difficult scenario because of the weather.

The first part of the mission involves intercepting the tanker. Once we have the tanker in sight, we each take positions on the wing of that tanker. When it is my turn to get a fill-up, I slip below and behind. The tanker is adorned with a series of red, green, and yellow strips of lighting. We are guided into refueling position by those lights. When all lights line up green, the boomer (refueling control person) sticks the refueling boom into our fuel nozzle and starts pumping.

Our four-ship formation of F-106 fighters are up to the task as each takes its allocated amount of jet fuel from the aging KC-135, a derivative of the old Boeing 707 and a workhorse for the Air Force for decades.

We split the formation into two pairs and continued to the next phase of our training mission. After a lengthy amount of flying, we head for home. I am the wingman as we recover to our home base.

Vertigo is a phenomenon whereby your body, your senses, tell you one thing about your aircraft's attitude, but the reality is different. It can be particularly harsh at night, and I am experiencing a major vertigo episode, as I am focusing my attention on the lead aircraft. My mind is telling me that our flight of two aircraft is in a steep turning dive. I glance down at my instruments and see that we are actually in straight and level flight. When I look back at the lead aircraft my senses tell me that he is turning sharply into me. I pull away in what I think is a level turn to reestablish the formation. But I am not turning level but am pulling up instead. I am clear of the lead aircraft, but when I look at my instruments, they show me in an almost vertical climb and losing airspeed quickly. I immediately look outside to find the horizon to right the airplane, but the stars and ground lights meld together, and I am further lost in my rapid climb. I watch the airspeed drop below 100 knots and head toward zero. These fighters just don't fly well at a low speed, and I was headed for my first ever hammerhead stall. I realized that any input into the flight controls might flip my aircraft into a spin, from which there is no recovery.

The solution... just let go of the control stick. I released the stick and became a passenger in this out-of-control jet. My mind started to race while I had nothing better to do. I started thinking. Hmmm...I am over the Olympic mountains... the mountains are very cold this time of year... hmmm...what is the altitude of those mountains... hmmm... did I put my survival suit on tonight? I watched the altimeter start falling; 30,000 ft, 25,000 ft, 20,000 ft. I remembered that our out-of-control ejection altitude was at 10,000 ft. Finally, the nose snapped down and I recovered at about 14,000 ft.

The rest of the flight was uneventful, but my heart was still racing even after I touched down. We all had a good laugh about it over a beer as I fessed up to my misadventure. It turned out I was not the only one with vertigo that night.

Chapter 6 – What Could Have Been

I had just finished the third grade at Fort Bragg, and we piled into the Ford.

It didn't seem like a big deal to the six of us. We were only on a trip to the city of Fayetteville, North Carolina, to look at a house. Mom was extremely excited, and Dad was ho-hum. Dad was preparing for an extended overseas assignment. He was being deployed to fight one of those secret wars. The question was: where would the family stay while he was deployed? Mom was hoping against hope that this house would become a home for the family. They were ready to sign the papers.

At the last moment Dad nixed the deal, squashed her dream, and this was the final straw that ruined their marriage. We were homeless.

The only thing she wanted was a home.

Mom and the six of us kids gathered what slim belongings we had, hopped into the old '53 Ford, and shuffled off to Buffalo again. This time it was different. Our parents were done as a couple, and we now had a single Mom with six kids and very few financial resources.

I do not remember much about the trip from Fort Bragg to Buffalo, and Grandma's house. In later years, my mom told me that she was so hopeless at that time, that she was ready to drive all seven of us over one of the many cliffs we passed while riding through the mountains of Virginia.

Grandma's rules had not changed. Four of us now took our places in the kitchen corners. Dana, no longer the prized child, joined us in a summer that seemed to last for years. Philip and Valerie were now Grandma's darling babies.

I remember Grandma's woodshed. It was a dark, dilapidated structure in the back yard. If you got overzealous or broke the rules you were sent to the woodshed. I spent a few days in the woodshed myself. I remember the smell of barbeque coming from the neighbor's yard. It was worse torture than the isolation and the rats. Food was scarce and there was hardly a day that we were not hungry.

We finally made the list to go to subsidized housing, a complex called the Perry Projects. Mom and the six of us settled in. I remember that my mom had a budget of

$200 coming from Dad's army pay. Even back then it was a pittance with her trying to feed and clothe six kids.

If you want to look at the results, it is amazing what my Mom produced. Of her six kids, three have college degrees, one a long-term bank manager, a 40-year tenured civil servant and a top-notch legal secretary. Most importantly... none in jail and none on the streets! But it did not come without some pain.

Mom ran a tight ship. As a single mom, with almost no financial resources, it was her way or the highway. Mental and physical abuse were commonplace. As the two oldest siblings, Alice and Gene took most of the physical abuse. Holes in the wall and broken furniture were evidence of the violence. I, the third of six, managed to keep an invisible profile and skated. The three youngest quickly learned the lay of the land.

I think my five siblings would agree that I was Mom's favorite. I couldn't wait to rush home with my report card and receive her approval. She always attended my big events and while at the Air Force Academy I could expect a letter from her every couple of days, with family news and words of encouragement. She was a great letter writer and an even better conversationalist. Neighbors and even classmates would come over and listen to her go on and on.

When Mom met my girlfriend Cathy, she warmly embraced her. Cathy's mom and my mother got along famously, and secretly speculated about when there might be a wedding. Mom loved our poodle "Pierre" and would let him lick her all over the face. When baby Aaron came along, she was a doting grandma. She never got to see Jordan, our second.

It was so hard to see her at my last visit, just Mom and me. She was worn out and defeated. She was embittered toward life. She felt like she got the short end of the stick... never had the chance to explore her own potential. Her life was "wasted." At that point she was skin and bones and would not even go to the doctor to get a diagnosis. Mom passed away at the young age of 59. Cause of death... unknown. But I think it was "failure to thrive." She had given all...with nothing left.

All she wanted was a home.

Thank you, Mom.

Up From the Projects

Chapter 7 – The Perry Projects

We lived on the eighth floor. There was an elevator, but it was always a mess, so we used the stairs a lot. It was good for the legs as we trudged up and down countless times a day. I remember riding up the elevator with Aunt Bert and Uncle Ed. They were relatives that brought an occasional food basket to the apartment. While visiting they passed around dimes to each of us kids as well as neighbor children. I cannot imagine their thoughts as we rode up that elevator together, dodging puddles of urine that were commonly present.

The projects were public housing, built for the unfortunate families that could not afford anything else.

That was us. The projects were in a neighborhood called the 1st Ward. It was a mixed bag of Italians, blacks, Irish - a potpourri of race and ethnicity, unlike other parts of Buffalo.

In Buffalo you had your Polish section, you had your Italian neighborhood, you had the Irish in South Buffalo, while the black population was in an area called Jefferson Street. The Jefferson Projects were the center of the deeply black populated area. It was an area no one white dared wander into. I remember once during a summer internship that I was mugged at a bus stop on Jefferson Street. I lost my bus money and had to walk home. But it could have been a lot worse. Fortunately, a big black man from a neighborhood bar came to my rescue and scared off the muggers.

We eventually moved up the food chain to a row house in the Perry Projects. It was a big step up, having cast off the urine-soaked elevators of the eight-story.

And it was there in the rowhouse of the Projects that my father showed up one afternoon: and he was "carrying!" The first thing I heard was a gunshot at the front door. I do not know what his intentions were, but I could only assume he was after the whole family. There was screaming and yelling and we, upstairs, were looking for a place to hide. Then things became eerily quiet, and we made our way down the stairs. The police were there, and 'dear old dad' (What the six of us called him) was nowhere to be seen.

It seems that dear old dad, experienced Army Green Beret with three tours in Vietnam, had accidentally shot himself in the leg. No purple heart to be had this time. Instead, he made an embarrassing trip to the Perry

Project office where he awaited an ambulance and the police. I had a chance to see him in that office before they hauled him off to the hospital. It was the first I had seen him in years and my heart was full of disdain for the man as I watched him bleed.

We never knew what his intentions were, but when he showed up at the front door my mother locked him out. He thought the butt of the gun might be a useful tool to break the lock and bang, bullet to the left thigh.

The press reports told it all, and it was a huge embarrassment to the whole family, as we had to explain it countless times to friends and other classmates. It could have been worse. We could have all been dead!

Chapter 8 – How I Learned to Become Invisible

It was my second year at South Park High School. We were sitting in our home room, waiting for the rotation of classes to begin that day. One of my classmates made a comment to the teacher, a compassionate woman who seemed to love her work. "Did you hear about Bruce Miller winning the 'Best Actor Award' last night?" "Are you talking about this Bruce Miller!?," she asked. "Yes, he won the award at the 'Hallow-one Night' play presentations last night." She looked at me with an incredulous glance and seemed flabbergasted. It seems that I had never said a word in her class the entire semester, and she must have thought that I had a speech defect. I didn't say anything... (that's a joke!)

The fact is that I learned to be invisible at an early age. I spent my early years in a family that was rocked by alcoholism. There were six kids, a caring and dedicated mother, and a raging alcoholic Army man for a father. We never knew what to expect when he rolled in late in the evening, but it was usually with anger on his mind and nowhere to vent it but in our house. It did not take long for me to figure out that with six kids as a target, the best strategy was to "disappear." Hence the cloak of invisibility that I developed.

While many people might have thought me "mildly autistic," it was my way of coping, and it served me well. I became non-verbal. Especially during key stress moments of my life.

Flash forward a few years. I am in basic training at the Air Force Academy. It is a mentally jarring experience, one that a large part of the population has experienced in basic military training. I was so unprepared. A 133-pound beanpole of a kid who didn't even know how to shave. We started in the morning with klaxons sounding off and upperclassmen pounding on our doors. We were hustled out to the terrazzo to begin our day with a several mile run, holding our M-1 rifle at the port position. Some of my classmates fell to the wayside along the way. Somehow, I managed to barely hang in with the formation day after day.

The rest of the routine included nonstop verbal and mental hazing. It was near enough abuse to make one want to quit the program, but my only other option was an embarrassing trip back to Buffalo with my tail between my legs. Hence my cloak of invisibility, I do not know how I made it. One day at a time was how I survived.

Fast forward to SERE training (Survival, Escape Resistance and Evasion). We spent the first week at a simulated POW camp, mostly a mental challenge since physical abuse was off the table. The upper-class cadets played the bad guys. It paled in comparison to the real thing. Later on, our fighter squadron welcomed Jack Butcher, a real POW who had been shot down in Vietnam and spent two years in the Hanoi Hilton, a moniker given to an infamous POW camp in North Vietnam. Jack never mentioned his two-year imprisonment. I am sure he carried some scars. I cannot even imagine what he went through. For me, however, it was nonetheless, a jarring experience. No problem, be invisible...attract the least attention.

The next two weeks involved being turned loose in the Colorado mountains. There were bad guys (upper class cadets) everywhere, so you had to escape and evade them, or you were thrown back into the POW camp. You have no food and a single live rabbit for each team of three. We had to live off the land. The three of us had to decide when to eat the rabbit. I had the unlucky draw to kill the rabbit: Grab him by the back feet and a sharp karate chop to the neck. We ate good that night, but one of the team (not me) had to eat one of the eyeballs.

Fast forward to Army airborne parachute school at Fort Benning, Georgia. Easy, my invisible cloak helped me through the harsh treatment once again.

I have never relinquished that cloak of invisibility. It has emerged time and time again, sometimes to my detriment.

Around a group of three or more people I tend to fade into the woodwork. Over the years some people may mistake me as an aloof and unapproachable character. Not so. It is just one of those traits that I have lived with over the years.

Nevertheless, we entertain a lot. Our house was and is often the party place. My wife, Cathy, does an excellent job of covering for me. I have been known to gulp down a shot of whiskey before the guests arrive to loosen up. Now, get me in a group of a hundred, or a thousand. That is where I feel most comfortable speaking out.

Chapter 9 – The Young Capitalists

Even kids can figure it out. When you're poor you look for ways to get unpoor. My younger brother Dana and I became a team as we scoured the neighborhood for ways to make a buck. Actually, small change would have been enough.

A fellow friend and classmate, James, had a gig. He made a little cash by shining shoes. Dana and I hooked up with him, learned the ropes and began our first career....shining shoes, boots, sneakers...whatever. Our price?...a measly 15 cents. Of course, we hoped for the tip...that's where the profit was. I was 12, Dana was 10.

Our clientele? The bars in our neighborhood...and there were plenty of them. We bought an ammo case at the local army surplus store, bootblack, brushes, and shining rags. We covered our expenses, plus a little extra. I remember one night, around Christmas, we entered Hagen's Bar with our ammo case and perused the bar for a new client. "Shine mister?...shine mister?" We ran into a couple of ladies who thought we were the cutest things. They sat us down at their table, bought us snacks and pop and let us shine their high heel shoes. We left the bar with a $5 tip. We were ecstatic.

It was a tough job and eventually we looked elsewhere. A neighbor friend had just quit working at Lomeo's Delicatessen, in the heart of the Projects. For us it was the primo opportunity, and we jumped at it. Here was the deal. We split the job into weekdays and weekends and rotated. It was work that never stopped. Cleaning floors, stocking shelves, manning the "Penny Candy Bar" and so many other arcane duties. The Penny Candy Bar was a popular display case that had about 30 different selections for the kids of the neighborhood. I remember one day I was at the "Bar," and the next minute I was on the floor laid out. A can had fallen from the top shelf and split my head open. Countless stitches later and with a partially shaved head, I returned to my duties.

And deliveries? Yes, we were the original Door Dash...with a twist. I can't remember how many cases of beer I delivered to the high rise (eight story building). Yes, we would put the 24-case brew on a dolly and walk it to the customer. We worked from 8 AM to 10 PM. For the weekday(M-F) job we got $20...for the weekend $12. Did I mention...that was not per day....no, that was for the week. Even back then, that was gross abuse of child labor, but in the Projects, you took what you could get, and regular rules did not apply. But we were happy to have the job.

I remember Al Lomeo, proprietor, would always make comments to me. "Miller, you're never gonna make anything of yourself." I never figured out if he was challenging me or verbally abusing me, but it did stoke my internal fire.

That lasted for a couple of years. Then we split the partnership and went our separate ways.

Chapter 10 – The Orange Spectacle

Our commanders would encourage us to take our aircraft on cross-country trips periodically. The purpose? To become more proficient, to gain confidence, to build hours, to learn in a less familiar environment.

Whatever the reason, I was off on a cross-country adventure this weekend. First stop, Buckley Field, a long runway, serving an Air National Guard unit in Denver, Colorado. That day I was wearing my orange flight suit. We had both green nomex flight suits and orange ones. Only members of the Air Defense Command had orange flight suits, so, wearing the Orange was "showing the flag," as it were... worn by only the best pilots in the Air

Force. (For you fighter pilots out there, it was just orange... nothing more.)

Now might be a good time to mention that when an F-106 lands, it is at a high airspeed, 150 Knots (about 170 mph). To help slow the aircraft, and to save brakes, a parachute is deployed.

When you are "cross-country," at a "foreign" field, the maintenance crews sometimes cannot repack your chute properly. Because of that it was not uncommon to execute a "no-chute" landing and rely on the brakes more.

I can't say I wasn't warned about flying into Buckley Field. It is at an altitude of 5,000. At that altitude, your ground speed is higher due to the thin air, which makes for a longer landing "rollout" after touchdown. Couple that with a cross-country tradition of "saving your chute" and you have a recipe for disaster if not handled with care. I was not as careful as I should have been that day.

I was flying into the traffic pattern that morning. From the control tower I hear, "Call Sign, Lima Kilo 12 you are cleared to land." It was a visual overhead approach, routine, and often used in clear weather conditions. I wanted to "save the chute," and as I was turning final approach, I noticed that my airspeed was a little too high. As I approached the runway I was carrying an extra 10 knots, so my touchdown point extended a good ways past normal touchdown. About halfway down the runway I realized I was not slowing down as fast as I should have. I pulled the parachute handle to slow the aircraft, but I was going too fast to stop by the end of the runway and too slow to get much effect from the parachute. At about 4,000 feet remaining of this 12,000-foot runway, I realized I was in trouble. I pressed hard on the brakes... perhaps a little too hard. BANG, I heard one tire blow. BANG, there went the other tire. I was in a world of hurt, knowing I could not stop before the end of the runway.

Suddenly a calm voice came over the radio. "You might want to use the cable, Lima Kilo 12." It seems the control tower was monitoring my dilemma and gave me the perfect out at the perfect time. I lowered my tailhook, and, thankfully, engaged the cable at the end of the runway. The wounded aircraft sunk into the gravel of the overrun, but at least I was alive and in one piece.

The maintenance team finally arrived with a ladder to help me out of the cockpit. As I exited the F-106, I was humbled... no I was humiliated by my lack of judgment. If flying cross-country was to gain experience, I got a good dose of it that day. My aircraft sat in the overrun with two blown tires, but otherwise, unscathed.

It took a good while to fix the situation. I had a wounded bird from the Air Defense Command, and I was a mere 60 miles away from the Headquarters of the Air Defense Command at Colorado Springs. How was I to fix this situation without attracting the attention and ire of my ultimate supervisors?

I proceeded very carefully. The crew at Buckley Field did an excellent job of jacking up the aircraft, putting it on two tractors and hauling it to the hangar.

My job was to call home with the bad news. Fortunately, my good friend, and groomsman Ken Galloway was the officer-in-charge that day and he handled the situation deftly and quietly. He sent another F-106 to Buckley in short order. It had two new tires on it for my wounded bird. That afternoon the Buckley Field maintenance staff changed the tires and, amazingly, I was good to go.

In the meantime, I spent the next eight hours that day at Base Operations, the area where all outgoing pilots prepare flight plans, a bright orange beacon of stupidity.

Chapter 11 – I Found My Voice

Public School No. 4, Buffalo School System: A strange way of naming schools. It especially comes into play when answering your security questions from your new secure computer application. **Name of Your Grammar School:** 4...? It just doesn't seem right!

But School 4 was where I matriculated. In the heart of the First Ward, it drew its student population from the mixed-race Projects and the pure white troublesome population of kids east of South Park Avenue.

When I entered the fourth grade, after our long journey from North Carolina, I was at the top of the class, academically speaking. My fellow students accepted me as such, and wrote it off as "coming from a military school." My inability to speak in class was not a factor. The quieter I was, the smarter my classmates thought I was. Sometimes silence is a good thing.

The teachers were a mixed bag. Most of them were good educators, but some belonged in a different profession. I will never forget my math teacher in seventh grade. His thing was to throw erasers. If you talked or misbehaved in class, expect a well-aimed eraser to knock you on the head. The frustrating part was that it was a wasted year because I already knew everything he tried to teach about math. I was relegated to staring out the window at the traffic light on the corner and trying to time out when it would go from green to orange to red. I wanted to learn, learn, learn. Instead, I was bored, bored, bored.

I remember one time the principal was touting the virtues of our school at an assembly, and she mentioned that we had students with an IQ as high as 156. She was looking directly at me when she made that comment. I really didn't know what that meant, but the number always stayed with me.

It was Graduation Day as I got up to give my valedictory address to the eighth-grade audience as the top student in the class, I was nervous, but extremely excited. It went well and I was so surprised that, although I could not function orally in the classroom setting, I loved speaking in front of a group of people. That would be one hallmark of my life. I went on to speak to hundreds of groups and sometimes thousands of people. Not bad for an autistic-like kid. I found my niche.

Chapter 12 - The Yellow Bus

Every Sunday morning it would show up at the Projects. It had the reputation of being the ride for "special children," those who were not right in the head. But most Sunday mornings we would hop on. It started with my oldest brother Gene. He had such an attitude-changing experience that we, his other siblings, took notice, and took the ride. Gene was a hot head. He was the dominant figure, rising a foot taller than the rest of us children. He was never wrong, and you risked a sharp physical response if you questioned his opinion. He believed that cheating was a part of any game and freely broke the rules. But after the bus rides, he mellowed out.

He was still difficult to deal with, but we all noticed the change.

Most everyone in the family took the ride at some point. It was to Faith Gospel Tabernacle, a small church on the west side of the city and about a thirty-minute ride. Faith Gospel was a fiery evangelical church in the Italian part of the city. I cannot say enough good things about the Mancini and Rizzo families that formed the foundation of the church. It was here that we all had our first religious experience. I maintained my "semi-autistic demeanor" through my days at Faith Gospel Tabernacle. But it was OK. I was learning about God, and it felt good.

Every Sunday morning, and sometimes on Wednesday evenings you could find Dan Mancini, Joshua Mancini, his younger brother, or Russell Rizzo, a brother-in-law, driving the bus and giving us a hearty welcome at the Projects. In hindsight, their efforts on our behalf were immense and I will be forever grateful. Wednesday night was the Youth Service, and we made some fast friends there.

Faith Gospel introduced us to "Youthtime," a Christian Recreation Center that had basketball, bowling, and other activities. We spent many Saturdays there and usually stayed for the "Youth Rally" that evening, an energetic religious service, with an altar call at the end.

When a regional rally would materialize, the yellow bus was once again our taxi. About 15 or 20 of us would pile in and we would have a great songfest along the two-hour drive. Some fantastic speakers would present the case for Jesus and one of them pierced my soul, and I committed my life to God.

I was so excited to no longer be alone, but to be able to call on God through the tumultuous happenings of the day. I knew that when my strength waned that my higher

power did not, and that knowledge has stuck with me

through all the phases of my life. I found my lifetime

verse at one of my later severe trials. Philippians 4:13: "I

can do all things through Christ who strengthens me."

Thank you, Lord, Amen.

Chapter 13 – The Painful Growth Spurt and Beyond

Looking at my eighth-grade graduation picture, it shows a 4-foot 6-inch munchkin walking across the stage, a full foot shorter than most of my classmates. How did that short slight individual, with an attitude, get to a point where he could compete for a Congressional Appointment to the Air Force Academy? Well, it was not that first year in high school! I was too busy growing. I was tired all the time with aching bones and muscles that were trying to adjust to a new form. I grew to 5-foot 8-inches that year and it was a painful process.

I was able to keep up with the academics, but activities took a back seat to fatigue. I did manage to join Junior Achievement. Junior Achievement, or JA, as it was called, is a program where high school students get together and form a company. They develop a strategy, create a product or service, and try to make it succeed in a one-year time frame.

That first year I was elected President of the new company that a random group of students put together. It was a foretelling of the significant role that JA would play in my life for the next four years.

After that I caught fire. Academically near the top of the class, I competed in the televised academic college bowl for South Park High School. I went on to win the Best Actor Award for two years running. I was in Honor Society, on the school newspaper, captain of the chess team, captain of an undefeated debate team. But my true focus centered around Junior Achievement.

We had a highly active JA program in Buffalo. The program had many other avenues of pursuit, including public speaking. There were local, regional, and national conventions for which you could qualify. Always a buzz of activities, the amazing group of participants helped me to work through my semi-autistic demeanor.

I was elected to be President of the local company for four straight years. I won numerous speaking awards. I was elected to be Vice-president of the Regional Convention, known as ROJAC, and President of the local convention for the Niagara Frontier. I was lucky enough to attend two national conventions in Bloomington, at the University of Indiana.

All of this happened in a little over two years. As my high school years wound down, I was selected as one of the Outstanding Teenagers in the nation, by the East Coast Explorers Council, and accepted the honor at West Point.

Then, as a senior, having accomplished so much in such a brief time, I experienced burnout. I grew tired of the academic grind and drew back from my activities, trying to figure out what my next steps would be. "Maybe I can be an athlete!" I thought. Hard to imagine!! But where there's a will...

I found an old tennis racket in the fall of my senior year. Not knowing a thing about the game, I went over to the dirt field behind St Bridget's, the old Catholic Parish. It strikes me as funny, in hindsight, to think about a tennis court in the Projects. Undeterred, I started hitting tennis balls against the brick wall of the parish. Day after day I would pound those tennis balls and chase them down as they ricocheted off dirt and stones of the open field.

Come springtime I went out for the South Park tennis

team and, surprisingly, I made it as a doubles team

member. You cannot imagine the pride I felt at the spring

sports award assembly. My one and only "letter," and

one of my most prized accomplishments. Imagine that:

the Projects spit out a tennis player.

And now the suspense. I apply.

I must have been enamored by my awards ceremony at

West Point earlier in the year. My father was in the Army,

and the facilities there were very impressive. It made

sense that it would be a fit for me. That is when luck took

hold.

I sent a letter to my congressman, the honorable

Thaddius J. Dulski, along with my impressive resume,

requesting his one and only appointment to West Point.

A few weeks later I would receive a letter from his office.

"Mr. Miller, thank you for your letter and resume. Unfortunately, I have already granted my appointment to another deserving student. Would you consider an appointment to the Air Force Academy?" I did not even know where the Air Force Academy was, but I grabbed the opportunity. It turned into an amazing blessing, but only after a difficult four-year journey.

Chapter 14 – We Almost Lost Her

I remember Mr. Gagliardi, the gym teacher from Public School No. 4. I was well into my high school years, but Mr. Galiardi was still the gym teacher there when my youngest sister, Valerie, was in the fourth grade. Today was the day he would become a hero.

But first let us go back to the neighborhood, where my older sister Alice was visiting our mother with her two young children. The hot coffee had been poured and was sitting on the table. Baby Michelle, my youngest niece at nine months old, grabbed it and pulled it towards her, spilling it over her body, and scalding her terribly. Michelle was wailing, her skin blistering, and needed immediate medical attention. Alice rushed Michelle to the hospital.

Back to School No. 4: The fourth-grade class was on a field trip to Chestnut Ridge Park. Chestnut Ridge is a large state park, near Buffalo. It has rolling hills, chasms, and ravines... a beautiful wonder of nature. When the bus hit the parking lot the kids piled out and were on their own for the day. Valerie and a group of her friends wandered around until they were totally lost. Valerie came up with an idea. "If I climb to the top of that ravine, I will be able to see our way out of the ravine and back to the group." Up went the 10-year-old climbing higher and higher, while her friends watched. When she got to the top of the hill she saw horses. Never having seen a real horse it scared the dickens out of her. Val started scrambling down the ravine, made totally of loose rocks. She saw what she thought was a tree and grabbed onto it for balance. Unfortunately, the tree pulled from the ground, and she fell backwards. Down she tumbled, one hundred feet down a cliff. She lost consciousness almost immediately but not before screaming long and loud enough to be heard at the picnic site where the class had assembled.

Our hero of this chapter, Mr. Gagliardi, ran towards the sound of the scream, enlisting the help of the school bus driver on his way. Valerie was found face down in a creek, unresponsive, bleeding from her chin (which had been torn open by the rocks), and having multiple lacerations.

Val woke up in the arms of Mr. Gagliardi. The first thing she did was spit out chunks of teeth that had been shattered on the way down the ravine. She next asked Mr. Gagliardi, "Am I dead yet?" Mr. Gagliardi tried to put Valerie down on her feet so she could walk out of the ravine on her own. She collapsed, having fractured her pelvis in numerous places. Thus, our heroes began the arduous task of taking turns carrying Val out of the ravine.

The bus driver ended up taking Valerie to the closest hospital. She remembers someone cradling her on the bus, and Val asked, "Who's going to pay for this?" It is always a concern for anyone raised in poverty.

Once Val arrived at the hospital, x-rays were taken and it was determined that not only did she have multiple pelvis fractures, but multiple fractures of the jaw, a concussion, and multiple contusions and lacerations.

Mom received a telephone call from the hospital that Valerie had had an accident and needed to get to the hospital right away. So... Mom made her way to the bus stop. Coincidentally, while our mother was getting ON the bus, my sister, Alice was getting OFF the same bus with news that Michelle had to be admitted to Children's

Hospital. While Mother was thinking Val's injuries were minor, she was in for a shock. She did not know she would be walking in to see her baby wrapped entirely in gauze, blood leaking from her chin and numerous lacerations.

Valerie was in traction for a month. I remember visiting her sometime later. She was totally bored and could not wait to get back to her life.

What more could go wrong that day? Don't ask. That evening the local channel blared breaking news. A large ship had exploded in Buffalo Harbor, killing several workers. Two of those workers were older sister Alice's good friends.

 A sad day all around.

Chapter 15 – The Blue Zoo

I did not get to attend my South Park High School graduation. The Air Force Academy was calling and would not be denied. Doolie (first year cadet) Training started before graduation rolled around. I was not as prepared as I should have been. I enlisted a trainer at the local public recreation center, and we prepped some basic running and calisthenics. You do not know what you do not know until you arrive at the storm that awaits. For example, I was a late bloomer, and, not having a father figure to provide guidance, I did not think about the fact that I had not yet started growing facial hair. I did not even bring a razor. If I had, I would not have known how to use it. A special heaping of verbal abuse and mockery resulted because of it. The humiliation was just the start of what would be a full year of hazing and intimidation. In looking back, it was just what every other person who has been through basic military training went through. Break them down, and reform them into a person who can function through the stress of military life.

My academic mastery was a thing of the past. I stumbled through the first year at the Academy with a 2.35 GPA, a "C" grade. Why? Because I never really learned good study habits in high school because everything had come so easily to me. That, coupled with the constant harassment, made me doubt if this was the right place for me.

So, I withdrew emotionally. I used my cloak of invisibility to get through. In my mind, no other options existed. I ground it out, one day at a time, for 1455 days (about 4 years). My leadership skills... my organizational skills... my hard-won public speaking ability, went dormant. I was in purgatory, waiting for what was next.

In the second year, with hazing behind me, I was able to focus more on my academics. Every year I got stronger. By the third year I was on Dean's List to stay. In my major, Engineering Management, I maintained a 4.0 GPA, until I ran into a professor who demanded class participation for an "A" grade. Remember that teacher in high school who was surprised by my acting career because I was so quiet? Same thing... same behavior. There was hardly a class where I participated orally. I tried to trick the professor into giving me an "A" grade by spending an entire Thanksgiving weekend preparing a 150-page monster term paper. To no avail, no classroom participation, no "A" grade. One class from perfection.

But good enough to qualify me for a follow-up MBA program.

81

Next was a quickie MBA program at UCLA, and then my new adventure, pilot training, which made all the past trials seem worthwhile. How I loved flying!!!

Chapter 16 – Excruciating WOW

A boy from the Projects does not have the experience of knowing that Florida sunshine is not something to be tampered with. It was my second summer at the Academy. One of the summer duty tours involved traveling to different Air Force bases around the country to get a feel for Air Force life. We headed to Tyndall Air Force Base, on the panhandle of Florida, to experience the Air Defense Command. Tyndall was a training base for fighter pilots. Our crew arrived on the weekend and had a couple of days to enjoy the Florida sunshine. I spent hours on the beach in my swimsuit, playing volleyball and other activities. I had no thought of the

Florida sunshine until Sunday evening, when my skin turned redder than a lobster. I was in so much pain I could hardly move. The problem was that I had an orientation flight in a fighter on Monday.

Believe it or not, getting sunburned was a punishable offense if it interfered with your duty. If written up, you might end up spending countless hours doing "tours" on the terrazzo, the beautifully laid out parade ground at the center of the Academy complex. A tour is a period when you march back and forth, in full regalia, with your rifle on your shoulder for an hour. It was a typical punishment for a violation of the rules.

So, do I go to the sick bay at the dispensary or suck it up, and go for the flight? Well, I was pretty determined to keep my record clean, so I headed for the flight line. I went through lengthy briefings from life support personnel. "Life support" is the part of the flight experience related to safety measures. You learn about how to work with your equipment during an aircraft emergency, including how to eject from an aircraft and what to do after an ejection.

The pilot who would be taking me on this flight gave his briefing next. This was to be my first time in a fighter jet, and oh, what a painful experience it was. The aircraft was an F-106B Mach 2 interceptor, something I would become very familiar with in my Air Force career.

When the life support people slipped the parachute over my flight suit, that covered stage three burned shoulders, I wanted to scream, but held it in. When I climbed into the cockpit, it got worse.

My pilot wanted to show me everything that aircraft could accomplish. All I wanted was out. We lit the afterburner and did an afterburner takeoff and climb.

That is where you keep the aircraft low to the ground, pick up as much speed as possible and then pull the nose up hard with a 5G climb out. I watched the ground and runway get smaller and smaller. It was an amazing experience, like being in a rocket. I was in awe, and I was in pain! It was a matter of WOW......OW.....WOW.....OW. We did all kinds of aerobatics and broke the sound barrier, past Mach 1, for my first time and finally headed back to the base.

Talk about a pleasure, pain experience! But I managed through it. Little did I know I would log a thousand hours of flight time in that aircraft.

Chapter 17 – Jumping Out of a Perfectly Good Airplane

It started over spring break of my second year at the Academy. Everyone was off, heading back home or taking a different type of vacation. I was strapped for cash, so I was one of the few cadets still hanging in the dorm. I had an idea. The Air Force allows free standby for active-duty personnel in their aircraft whenever space allows. I thought, "let's see how far I can get on free hops." I could use the lodging at the destination base, so basically, free vacation! I headed to Peterson Field, the Air Force base nearest the Academy and checked flight itineraries. Sure enough, there was a flight headed to Florida. I hopped on.

When I hit Florida, I checked the itineraries again and found a flight to Hanscom Field, outside of Boston. I remembered that my father was stationed at Fort Devens, Massachusetts, a short distance from Boston. Out-of-the-blue I decided to drop in on "dear old dad," whom I had not seen since the infamous day in the Perry Projects. It was like meeting a new person. He took my surprise in stride, and we hung out together for a few days. I found that perhaps he was not the monster that my mother had relentlessly trained us to think he was, but I never did get the back story.

One of my first memories of him was stuffing gobs of peanut butter down my throat, when I was three or four, until I threw up. We were always hungry, and I tried to take some extra food on the sly. Hence, my punishment.

I remember the alcohol induced fits that came late in the evening after bedtime. But I also remember good times.

My Dad patiently taught me how to play chess when I was a young child. My goal was to eventually beat him at chess. One day I ended up at the hospital when I was eight years old. It was a polio scare because my legs quit working one morning. My Dad showed up one afternoon with a chess board. Finally, I had my chance. To no avail... beat again! The polio scare turned out to be a tick bite and I healed quickly.

We talked and talked for days, during that spring break visit, and then he said, "Want to play chess?"

I casually told him about my summer program selection, parachute training at Fort Benning, Georgia, the same place he had earned his Airborne Wings. He said, "I will see what I can do." I did not know what that meant, but we said our goodbyes and I found other free flights back to Peterson Field.

Flash forward to Fort Benning and parachute or Airborne training.

Don't ask me why. I guess I just like to punish myself. Here I am at Fort Benning, Georgia, being mentally abused and constantly harassed. They had a few extra spots at Army "jump school" and let Air Force Academy cadets choose this as a training option during summer break.

I must have thought I could use the training someday and boy was I right.

It was a rigorous four-week training program, with five parachute jumps after which you were rewarded with your permanent "Airborne Wings," to wear with your other uniform awards and qualifications.

There was a surprise twist to my program. My father researched the timing of the training event and decided to make his way down to Fort Benning, some 25 years after his first parachute training at the same base. He was nearing retirement and wanted to make one final jump.

Our training would not allow for casual breaks for visitors, so I did not see him until he stepped on board the C-119 Boxcar, an old double boom propeller cargo aircraft, refitted for paratroopers. My platoon prepared to make our last jump, and he was to join us. It was quite a surprise since we had been estranged for most of my life until our recent spring break reunion. But it was incredibly special in hindsight.

The C-119 was to make one special pass prior to the group platoon jump, with only three jumpers. The Base Commander was set to jump first; my father would go next to celebrate his last jump in the Army; and... You guessed it, I would be the third and last, celebrating my qualifying jump and completion of training.

You might ask: What was going through my mind during this heavily publicized event that drew the attention of the local and regional press, "Father and Son jump together on final/qualifying jump"?

Fact is, I was just as scared for this fifth and qualifying jump as I was for the first four. Surely, I just lucked out when those first four parachutes opened, and my luck might have run out this fifth and final time!

Out I went!!! Poof... lucked out again as that parachute blossomed.

When I hit the ground the newspaper reporters were there to welcome me, but I was just so thankful to be alive and on the ground that I ignored the hoopla, gathered my chute, and met up with the rest of the trio.

What an experience!

Chapter 18 – It's a Boy!!!!

Long before I was the father of two amazing sons, I find myself assigned to Thailand for an orientation tour. It is the height of the Vietnam war. I was assigned to the 6010th Wild Weasel Squadron. They flew the F-105 Thunderchief, also known as the "Lead Sled", "Thud", as well as many other less respectful nicknames. It was a fighter/bomber with a special mission. Before I left, I was lucky enough to hitch a ride in that amazing aircraft.

My sponsor at Korat was a "Thud" pilot. He had a few close calls evading Surface-to-Air Missiles (SAMs) during his tour. A few months later he wrote me a letter at the Academy and told the story of how his wingman got hit with a SAM and parachuted out, only to land in a bamboo field, his body pierced as he landed onto the bamboo. Fortunately, they rescued him and treated his many wounds.

Korat Air Force Base in Thailand was a twenty-four hour buzz of activity in support of war operations. Aircraft headed for the war were launched from Korat hour after hour. It never stopped. The Officers' Club never closed. The bands at the club never stopped playing because the pilots were flying at all hours of the day and night and needed to blow off steam from the intense war experience, whether it was noon, 7 PM or 3 AM in the morning. For me, as a twenty-year-old cadet on a special summer program called "Third Lieutenant," it was incredibly mind bending.

Luckily, an old high school friend, Louie, had spent a couple of tours at Korat Air Force Base as a maintenance technician. He was familiar with the lay of the land and knew a lot of the locals. I had the opportunity to enjoy the peace and beauty of the incredible countryside, including visits to local national parks. This was just a couple of hundred miles from where the war was raging.

One weekend Louie took me to the red-light district of Korat City. Apparently, this was a "rite of passage" for everyone assigned to Korat. We entered the brothel and were told to pick our favorite from a glassed room. I picked an extremely attractive young lady, and we proceeded to the back. What followed was a bath and then an amazing massage of every part of the body. I had never experienced anything like it, before or after. Once the massage was over, she snuggled up to me and I was expecting even more of a treat. And then she said the dreaded words. Do you know 'Ka-toy'? And I did! I had been warned. I gathered my clothes, dressed as fast as I could and headed for the exit. Luckily, I had paid in advance. I did not need any more embarrassment!!

95

You see, a 'Ka-toy' is an attractive young man, dressed up and made to look like this extremely attractive young girl. Needless to say, I did not have a "Happy Ending."

Without a doubt, this was the highlight of my four-year tour at the Air Force Academy. Not the massage... The war experience in real time.

Chapter 19 - Can I have your number?

It was a Christmas party that everyone was expected to attend. It was put on by one of the commanders. I did not mind. I always enjoyed those types of get-togethers. I had to be careful, however. I was flying to Klamath Falls the next morning for a two-day alert tour. One of the key mantras of a pilot is "twelve hours bottle to throttle." That means if you were going to a party, with alcohol present, you had to track your takeoff time the next day to ensure the twelve-hour rule was enforced. It generally meant showing up for the party and making an early departure.

It was a particularly frustrating drive to the party. It was in a remote area, where the streets stopped and started on a whim. There was no navigation in the car back then and I was having a challenging time. By the time I found the address, I was in a foul mood from the driving experience.

I walked into the house and introduced myself all around. Then, as I was walking to the living room, I passed the kitchen and glanced inside. I saw the most beautiful girl I had ever seen attending to the needs of the party organizer, prepping food plates and playing hostess. She was very busy, but when she took a break, I sidled up to her and struck up a conversation. It was not long before I got to the part about asking for her phone number. She said no. Imagine that! Her saying no to the most handsome man in the house! I was taken aback.

It was almost time for me to say goodnight to the host, with my impending flight the next morning. I was trying to figure out a strategy to see that girl again because I knew that if I left, it would never happen. I started asking around and found out she was one of the neighbor's daughters and her parents were also at the party. I quickly introduced myself to her mother and shared some pleasantries. I explained to her my dilemma... having to leave early... hoping to see her daughter again. Could she help? She looked me up and down, got out her pen and wrote Cathy's number on my hand.

That night, when I got home, I was lying in bed watching the beautiful sky through a bedroom window. Suddenly, I noticed the biggest star I had ever seen illuminating the sky. Surely it must be a sign I thought. Could she be the one?

The next day, I called her from the alert barn and set up a date for when I got back. I took her to the Officers' Club, and we had a wonderful time together. I was dating a couple of other girls at the time, but it did not take long before both Cathy and I cast off our worries about the age difference (I was 6 years older), and I became a one-woman man.

We were married eight months later. We just celebrated our 47th anniversary.

Later in life, I became an amateur astronomer and now believe that I had actually seen Jupiter that night, brighter than all the stars in the sky at certain points. But I like my first story better.

Chapter 20 - The Memorial Day Miracle

It was a warm Memorial Day as Flight Lead Jack Butcher, and I prepared for the long trip to Florida. The mission today was a routine cross-country flight of two F-106 fighter aircraft from the home base of McChord Air Force Base in Washington State to Tyndall Air Force Base, Florida, where we were to participate in a live missile firing exercise. As I mentioned previously, the F-106 is a single seat, single engine fighter capable of speeds of more than 1500 miles per hour. Today, however, we would cruise to our midpoint stop at about 550 knots, the best airspeed for long distance flight. Actually, it was not a stop, but there was to be a KC-135 tanker, which would be refueling us over the skies of Oklahoma. Jack and I had flown in formation before. An ex-POW from the Vietnam War and highly experienced fighter pilot, Jack was a cool confident leader. I anticipated a smooth enjoyable flight across the country that day. But the flight was to last for less than a minute, its impact to reverberate for years.

Jack briefed us on the flight itinerary and the process for today's mission. We picked up our parachutes, helmets, and gear at the life support station... then hit the flightline to pre-flight our jets. The crew chief stored our luggage in my aircraft's internal missile bay. After entering the cockpit, we fired up our engines. Jack led the flight of two aircraft through the various radio frequencies, picking up the required clearances and we began our taxi to the runway. From the control tower radio frequency I heard, "Call Sign Lima Kilo Zero Two... cleared for takeoff," and we turned onto the runway. All cockpit indications were normal as we made our final emergency engine runup checks. At that point I focused on Jack's helmet in the lead aircraft. Hand signals and head nods are the language of formation flying, to keep the always busy radio chatter to a minimum. I am looking for that first head nod that would set the flight in motion. The first head nod indicates brake release. The second would be the afterburner light. The afterburner is a supplemental fuel control that provides a massive amount of additional fuel to the F-106, required during critical phases of flight like air-to-air combat and takeoff. My job was to keep a good tight formation position throughout the takeoff. The first head nod... then the second...The momentary loss of thrust, followed by the familiar explosive kick in the pants indicated that the afterburner engaged, and we were on our way. My eyes jumped from inside the cockpit to outside as I jockeyed the throttle to maintain good position. At 140 to 150 knots Jack lifted his aircraft nose to the takeoff position and I followed suit, noting that I was drifting slightly behind. I advanced the throttle to maintain position. The aircraft lifted off at what must have been 190 knots. When I saw Jack's head nod again, indicating gear up, I slapped the gear handle to the up position and felt the gear retract.

Then an urgent call came over the control tower's emergency radio frequency. "Kilo Zero Two wingman... it appears you're on fire!" I looked into the cockpit and heavy smoke billowed from the floorboards. Flashing emergency warning lights confirmed a pilot's worse fear: fire on takeoff.

Once the landing gear begins to retract there is no turning back. The fighter is committed to flight. There is simply no time to get the gear back down and catch the cable at the end of the runway.

Time began to slow down - ever so slow - as my mind sped up to evaluate the situation and my options. First, I cleared myself from my flight lead. The checklist calls for an immediate ejection in that scenario for fear that the airplane would explode, but I had a bigger problem... where the aircraft was headed and what it would hit when it crashed. The runway which we were departing from faced heavily populated South Tacoma. I knew that I could not let the aircraft fall into that area and I had a gut feeling that the intensity of the fire would prevent me from getting the aircraft around and back to the runway.

I started a right turn to the east. Having flown in the area for three years and being familiar with the terrain and population centers, I went with the odds. Parkland and Spanaway were sparsely populated areas compared to

South Tacoma and there were several open areas, including a large lake called Spanaway Lake. I hoped I could find one of those areas and get out before the impact. At that point I made my only radio transmission, accented with the uncertainty of my fate. "Jack, I'm on fire. I'm going to try to get out of here." I continued my turn and time slowed even more. I smelled a strong pungent odor which I later would recognize as JP-4, the jet fuel which feeds the engine, or in this case fed the flames. I feared the F-106 was ready to explode. As the smoke became thicker, I focused my attention outside the cockpit. The fumes were so strong that they overpowered the oxygen mask, in spite of the fact that I was breathing 100 percent oxygen. The ground sped by, and as I looked ahead, I was much lower than I had anticipated and try as I might, I was too close to the ground and moving too rapidly to predict an impact area.

I was in a 60-to-80-degree bank, only a few hundred feet from the ground. In my mind I hollered: "I need more time!!!, I need more altitude!!!" I attempted to roll the aircraft out of its bank, but the control stick became unresponsive as the fire had burned through the flight controls. I knew that I was close to, or past the limit of the ejection envelope, but I also knew that things were not going to get any better.

The F-106 was equipped with an amazing ejection system. So good that if a pilot ejected on the ground, he would be fired 200 feet into the air and have a parachute. The problem is that the ejection will fire you in the direction the aircraft canopy is pointed, and I was rapidly going over on my back, with controls frozen in a right-hand bank. I would very soon be fired into the ground.

I considered the fate of other aviators in the moments just before a crash and I feel that panic does not set in as long as there is the slightest amount of control that can be called upon or the slightest chance of rescuing the situation. In less than a second the decision was made. The instincts of training filled the gap that rational thought processes could not cope with, and I reached down and pulled the two ejection handles.

Surprisingly, I was totally without fear as I watched things unfold. I assumed the role of a casual observer to the dire situation knowing that unless every system worked perfectly that I would impact the ground before the parachute opened. I remember thinking…" so this is how people feel just before they die." I was in the hands of God as never before.

The canopy blew off the fuselage and I felt the rush of the wind. I experienced the crush of the rocket powered ejection seat hurling me out of the aircraft. As I left the aircraft my helmet, oxygen mask and all, was ripped from my head. I was weightless for what seemed like too long and when I felt the flap of cloth or some other material against my face, my thoughts raced through the possibility of a tangled chute. Then I felt the comfort of the opening parachute shock. Finally, I saw that big, beautiful orange and white canopy above my head and experienced a short-lived sense of relief.

Chapter 21 - The Memorial Day Miracle – Part 2

I had just ejected from this out-of-control fiery inferno at a couple of hundred feet. I was calmly waiting, almost like a disinterested observer, for either a fatal impact into the ground or... and there it was... that beautiful sound and feeling of the opening parachute shock.

When I stabilized in the parachute, I was pointed in the direction of the massively flaming aircraft just a few hundred feet in front of me. I watched as the plane was not flying anymore, but was in a stall, falling tail first. I watched as the aircraft plunged into a grove of trees in an otherwise sparsely developed area. Terror gripped me because I knew that a well-ordered group of trees would have a house under it and that a family would be sleeping in on this Memorial Day holiday. The flaming aircraft with 24,000 pounds (3,500 gallons) of jet fuel would create an inferno! The terror would remain awhile.

Those sights and thoughts came during the first swing of the chute. With the second swing came my ground impact, which I anticipated a split second early. I executed a perfect parachute landing fall, a planned fall and roll to distribute the shock of landing. It was something I had learned at Airborne School, at Fort Benning, Geogia. I landed in the middle of Steele Street, a well-traveled road just outside the base. Fortunately, it was quiet due to light holiday traffic.

A passing motorist immediately came to my aid, helping me take off my parachute harness as the rumbling of terror in my mind temporarily disabled my thinking

processes. I was in shock, trying to comprehend what

had happened, and what more tragedy was to come. I

was already reliving an experience that would not let me

rest for some time.

Moments later, as my mind briefly cleared, I had a

disturbing thought. My wife, of only eight months, lived

in our duplex, only a few miles from the runway and a

mile from the crash site. She would often listen for the

afterburner blast of an F-106 takeoff, and she knew Jack

and I were the only mission for that holiday morning. I

envisioned a panic reaction if she had seen or heard the

crash. What to do? I rushed to an old trailer along the

road, knocked on the door and burst through when it was

opened, not caring that I was disturbing the family inside

and not knowing whether I had even asked. I managed

to dial our phone number as some small, wide-eyed children in pajamas peeked around their bedroom door looking at what must have been a strange creature to them, with my flight suit, G-suit, and crazed manner. I greeted my recent bride with "Cathy, my aircraft caught on fire, I crashed but I'm OK. Goodbye!" I abruptly hung up the phone, not waiting for a response.

Then I am back on the street, watching events unfold. Sirens were wailing. Not towards me, but to the inferno which I knew the aircraft I had been piloting moments before created. I felt desolate and afraid. I was escorted to the shelter of a passing auto and as I sat in the passenger seat, I began to talk to God. "Lord, I pray that there will be no injuries coming out of this."... "Lord, I pray that there will be no injuries coming out of this." I prayed the same prayer again and again. My faith was not great at that moment. How can you pray for something that has already occurred... that you have already seen happen? Can God turn back time? But I prayed and prayed until a paramedic ambulance arrived and began to examine me.

I asked a police officer about casualties. He told me the aircraft had impacted a structure. Another person mentioned a parking lot, but no word of casualties yet. I was sitting in the ambulance when, out-of-the-blue, a familiar face appeared in the doorway. It was Doug Henning from my church, Peoples Church of Tacoma. Doug worked for Peoples Church as a counselor. He had been our marriage counselor a short 10 months earlier. How Doug showed up I will never know, but his presence somehow comforted me. Another surprise... a fellow F-106 pilot, who was also my flight commander (immediate supervisor), Major Ken Dean, was also on the scene and peaked into the ambulance. He lived only blocks away and had heard the crash.

Finally, the Air Force ambulance whisked me away to the Air Force clinic at McChord AFB, where a complete physical was accomplished. I asked the examining Air Force doctor about casualties. He mentioned that he had heard of none. I implored him to keep nothing from me and he responded that his ethics would not permit him to keep any distressing news from his patients and "besides" he said, "I'd rather you go into shock now with the medical facilities available rather than later." Once again, I was comforted.

The physical exam indicated no injuries except for light skin burn from the parachute straps. I left the dispensary and waited outside for Cathy's arrival. After my call, Cathy phoned her sister. She was too emotional to drive herself to the base, so she asked her sister JoAnne Still to pick her up. The two of them drove to McChord Air Force

Base and had to wade through a crush of reporters at the main gate. They picked me up at the dispensary, and we headed back to the squadron operations building, where the flight had begun just a couple of hours earlier.

The General and all high-ranking supervisors were waiting for a debriefing at the rapidly assembled accident board. As I recounted the story, my sister-in-law (sitting behind me) recounted that she saw the hair on the back of my neck standing up as chills ran through my body and tears welled up in my eyes. The chills were unresolved fears, the tears were thankfulness.

Satisfied that I had contributed as much as possible to the emergency accident board, my Commander, Lt/Col Lee V Greer told me to "Go upstairs and write it up." After I presented my debriefing notes to the boss, he barked: "Captain Miller, you are dismissed!" He was not happy he had just lost a jet!

Cathy and I drove home. As we traveled through the base the smell of jet fuel once again filled my nostrils and I recognized the scent as that pungent odor which I had experienced earlier in the cockpit. We drove by the spot where my parachute had landed. The traffic jam had since dispersed. When we arrived home, we turned on the noon day news program and listened to the story of the "Miracle Jet Crash" being broadcast. My mind at last found total release when it was disclosed that there was not a single casualty.

My prayers had been answered. There were no deaths. There were no injuries. Only the presence of God forming a protective shield over everyone involved.

"Get ready," I told Cathy. I changed out of my flight suit into civilian clothes. An hour later we were at the crash site. As I pressed through the crowds and support workers beginning the long cleanup operation, I began to fully realize the dimensions of the miracle that God had wrought.

When I was in my parachute watching the fiery F-106 plunge into what I thought was a small grove of trees with a home under it, I was actually seeing it fall into a large grove of trees.

The aircraft had come straight down through that grove of trees into the center of a small mud pond in the middle of an apartment complex. When the aircraft impacted the pond, the mud and water suppressed the intensity of the explosion, and fire which followed. Standing by the pond and looking in a 360 degree circle the only thing to be seen were apartments. I was totally encircled by two-story structures filled with families... All of them sleeping in on that holiday morning.

Three hundred people were living in the apartments. The

only way the F-106 could have come in was straight down. If it had had an angular vector (if it were still flying, and not in a stall) it would have impacted one or more of the buildings. The spread of the twenty-four thousand pounds of jet fuel could have engulfed much of the complex. The potential for disaster had rarely been matched. As I approached an Air Force Security Guard, I had to ask. "How did you build a chain link fence around the crash site so quickly?" "Mister," he said (not knowing I was the pilot of the doomed flight). "We didn't build that fence, the airplane crashed inside of it."

The mud pond was being renovated and the chain link fence was put up to keep out tenants. Contractors, who would have normally been working at the time of the crash, were off for the holiday.

I was on a natural high all day. It was good to be in the hands of a watchful and merciful God. I did not sleep well for many nights, but I was flying again in four days. The anxiety was there as I began takeoff roll and lit the afterburner. But the presence of God in my life calmed the fears, and I had the realization that if I can't handle it, God can!

Chapter 22 – Memorial Day Miracle Aftermath

It is interesting to watch an accident board investigation. The first thing that they do is remove the wreckage and attempt to piece back together the aircraft. In my accident, that meant they had to dig into the mud pit inside the pond where the F-106 had crashed.

If you recall, they had me flying again on the Friday after my Monday crash. The theory is "get him back on the horse as soon as possible," to quash insecurities that might emerge.

I flew to Kingsley Field for an alert barn tour. The newly inserted alert schedule was in part to get me away from the press. They would <u>not</u> allow the press to interview me, but the higher-ups <u>would</u> allow me to write to the press on my interpretation of the events, which I did. I did not expect the Tacoma News Tribune to do much with it, but the next day they printed it on the front-page word for word. My article was a testament to God's grace in the event. I was touched that they printed it.

On Saturday, while I was still on alert duty at Kingsley Field, they pulled the bottom of the wreckage out of the muck. Remember when I said that Jack and I were going cross-country to Florida? Well, you must put your luggage somewhere, and somewhere (for both Jack and I) was in the missile bay (a closed compartment for armament) of my F-106. In the luggage they found two Bibles, one in Jack Butcher's luggage, and, of course, my own, a wedding gift from my wife. Does that tell you anything?

My Bible is still readable, and I keep it as treasured keepsake; a symbol of God's mercy and glory.

Fast forward a few weeks. I was called in front of the accident board. But it was not a jaw tightening, grilling interview. It was a courtesy to me. They explained what they had found in their investigation.

The engine of F-106 #059-0144 had just finished a thorough rebuild. One of the measures they take is to x-ray the tail cone for cracks and weld the cracks when they find a problem. Mine was the first operational flight after the rebuild.

When I lit the afterburner that day, one of the repaired welds failed and redirected flame into the engine accessory compartment and caused the afterburner fuel control to explode. According to witnesses, when my afterburner lit that day, it was twice the flame of Jack's (my lead). It was clear to everyone on the ground that I had a big problem. But no one was near a radio to alert me to abort the takeoff. As the aircraft rolled, it was spitting parts onto the runway. I was firmly glued to my flight lead and had no notice that my plane was breaking up.

As I turned the aircraft to the east to try and clear populated South Tacoma, the fire approached the cockpit. The tower controller can be heard to say, "HE'S DYING!!, HE'S DYING!!;" then, "Tower, he's punching out, he's punching out."

The accident board confirmed that when I ejected, the force of the ejection caused my aircraft to flip into a post stall gyration. The F-106 went from flying to falling (in a full stall), tail first. It was falling, and it did not have an angular vector, so plummeted straight down through the trees, and directly into the center of the pond, confirming what I had witnessed in my parachute.

The accident board commended my actions. It felt good!

Chapter 23 - The Miracle Child

It was another drag on day. It is a matter of putting your time in when you are searching for the right career that has not really been invented. And so, you search for the right fit, looking at various opportunities that seem to fit, but you know are not quite right.

And then the phone rings. It is Cathy with that all-too-familiar panic in her voice. We are six months along on this journey. It has taken a major surgery to get her this far, but it still seems way too soon, and we are now looking at failed pregnancy number five... or so it seems.

Cathy's mom took a special drug called DES during her pregnancy with Cathy which, after the fact, was determined to create a problem in the female body known as an incompetent cervix. After so many failed attempts, we were thinking that children were out of the question. Then an ingenious gynecologist invented a cervical cerclage, where the cervix was stitched together once a viable pregnancy was established. The idea was to keep the cervix from rupturing during the pregnancy and delivering the baby at nine months via a C-Section.

Cathy's call was an indication that we had a severe problem. Our backup plan was Oregon Health Sciences University, or OHSU, an institution known for forward thinking in terms of neo-natal practice. Off we go, Cathy in labor at six months, not knowing what to expect, but fearing the worst.

After nine days of lying in her hospital bed, taking drugs to help ward off the labor, and more drugs to give the baby a chance to speed up lung development, Cathy's labor could be stalled no more. We were counseled through those nine days that the baby could be underdeveloped or have breathing issues. The eyesight is one of the last to develop and there was a chance if he survived, he might be blind. The question we were asked: "If the baby is severely deformed, do you want us to take extraordinary measures to keep it alive?" We prayed for the baby during those days. For us it was an easy decision. We trust that God will deliver us a baby and we accept him for whatever that blessing might entail.

Aaron entered the world in the wee hours of the morning on March 5, 1985. He was immediately whisked off to the neo-natal part of the hospital, but not before giving us a couple of cries, which immensely boosted our spirits. Aaron weighed in at 1 pound, 13 ounces. He was smaller than a beany baby and was the smallest male baby born at the hospital to that point.

Despite his small size, he turned out to be quite a fighter. He was breathing on his own from the start and never needed a ventilator as most of the wee ones in the room did. He seemed to have all parts in order, but it would take a couple of weeks for him to open his eyes. There were issues along the way as his weight dropped to 1 pound 8 ounces. They inserted a catheter into his heart to provide the sustenance he needed to survive.

We were so sad to see other parents holding their babies, knowing that their child had but a brief time to live. And there were those babies that would carry lifetime disabilities into the world. Plenty of tears flowed for those poor souls.

But Aaron thrived on the wonderful care and attention he was given by the amazing nurses in the neo-natal intensive care unit and prayers that were being offered up all over the world. We became fast friends with many of the nurses, as we trekked up the hill nightly to OHSU for the next two months.

Aaron became a poster child for the skill and ingenuity of the OHSU neo-natal program, and we will always be thankful for God's answers to our prayers.

We brought him home on May 5th, a full three weeks before his due date, a tiny, but healthy baby boy.

Praise be to God!

Chapter 24 – A Calm in the Storm

How did we do it? How are we still doing it? I love doing it.

Eight months from meeting to mating. It has been an adventure.

I remember walking into a restaurant the other day and a leaving patron said, "oh, look, they're still holding hands." We get that a lot.

Cathy has been there since day one. At first, the age difference (six plus years) made us both doubt if it was meant to be. But it <u>was</u> love at first sight.

Do we have the perfect marriage? Nobody does. Like everyone else, it took some adjusting. Through the years we have had our ups and downs. But she has always been there for me, and I hope that goes both ways. We are equal partners in life.

One of the things we share is a passion for travel. Honeymoon plans originally included a drive from Tacoma to Disneyland. I changed it up at the last minute, booking a trip to the three major islands of Hawaii. Our five-year anniversary included buying a Euro-pass and sightseeing through Europe. Then we were hooked. Argentina, Peru, Ecuador, the Galapagos Islands, Panama, Costa Rica, France, Spain, Germany, Denmark, Sweden, Finland, Russia, Estonia, China, Africa, Australia, New Zealand, Tahiti, Puerto Rico, the Carribean Islands, and others...always looking for new adventures.

Raising our two sons, Aaron, and Jordan.... She was the rock! I was always off to work, off on speaking engagements, or doing charitable work. I did my best under the circumstances, coaching soccer and baseball, helping with the Boy Scout troop, and heading up the PTA at our sons' school. I figured, if I was to be there anyway, why not make a difference.

Cathy is a social butterfly, a great conversationalist... making up for my sometimes social awkwardness. It's OK, it works for us.

Her passion is creating culinary masterpieces day after day. With a library of cookbooks, she is always experimenting with innovative ideas. I do not know how I manage to keep the weight off given her sumptuous offerings.

I am so thankful she came into my life that Christmas season way back. Here is to more travel, more adventures and more "doing it!"

Chapter 25 – And Then There Were Two

My commitment was up. I owed the Air Force eight years in return for my Academy education and the follow-up training. In 1980 it was time to move on. I knew I had a bright future out there and I was ready to explore my options. The only thing was... I loved flying fighter jets!

The Pacific Northwest had become my home, and I was committed to having and raising my family there. I knew that Oregon had the only other fighter squadron in the Pacific Northwest, so I thought "why not explore my options while continuing to serve my country." The Oregon Air National Guard was the perfect fit. After extended interviews they snapped me up. I was thrilled to get back into the cockpit.

I was honored to be able to fly the F-4 Phantom. It was a jet I admired and fantasized about my whole career. It was an aged design that would quickly be succeeded by third generation fighters like the F-15 Eagle and the F-16 Falcon, but what a great machine. The only problem... it came with a back-seater.

The back seater... affectionately known as the GIB (guy in back) ... technically known as the WSO (Weapons Systems Officer) ... also called the Navigator. I called him... a pain in the ass!

Don't get me wrong. These men were highly trained and, for the most part, easy to get along with, but the few with an attitude... they were hell to work with!

OK… I was a little spoiled. For most of my flying career I was a single seat pilot, accomplishing the same thing as this two tandem team. I wasn't keen on having someone else in the cockpit trying to control some aspects of the flight experience. But it came with the territory.

I got sidetracked from my life mission for a while. I became what they called "a guard bum." I made a living flying the F-4 and pulling 24-to-forty-eight-hour alert shifts to make a full-time wage (same thing I was doing in the Air Force). Fortunately, I continued my educational pursuits, picking up a second master's degree from Portland State University to add to my MBA from UCLA.

The flying was tame compared to my dramatic career in the F-106. One day the hydraulics on my Phantom ruptured, leaving me with limited flight controls and zero braking capability. Fortunately, the airport had just installed an arresting cable at the approach end of the runway (like the one I needed at Buckley Field in a prior adventure), and I would be the first pilot to try it out. It was similar to what you think of when you watch aircraft carrier landings. The Navy pilot slams his aircraft onto the deck, catching one of three cables that brings the fighter to rapid stop. I only had one cable to catch, but if I missed it, I could always execute a touch and go and come around for another try. Fortunately, the first approach was perfect, and we came to a screeching halt. I shut the engines down and we were towed back to the flight line.

Another first.

And then... the world as I knew it fell apart!

Chapter 26 – It Came Back to Haunt Me

Just like any other training flight... This time I am in my F-4 Phantom, that Mach 2 second generation fighter we talked about earlier. Little did I know that this routine flight would affect the direction of my life. It was something I never could have imagined.

My backseater was Dick Peterson. He was one of our best Weapons System Officers, or WSO(Wizz-O), as we used to call them. A WSO was responsible for all the avionics and radar systems, for finding and tracking hostile threats.

Dick and I were at about 30,000 feet that day and our Tactical Control Center found a low-level target for us to find and simulate destruction. The cloud formations looked oddly familiar. I did not think much of it at the time.

I told Dick we would Split S down to the ocean floor. A Split S maneuver is a half loop. You turn the aircraft on its back and pull through the second part of a loop, losing a huge amount of altitude in a short time.

I flipped the aircraft on its back. As I rolled, I noticed those oddly familiar clouds. Suddenly, I was back in that F-106, aircraft number 59-0144, in a similar attitude to that fateful flight from 6 years earlier, the Memorial Day Miracle flight. I immediately recovered the aircraft to level flight. My head was swimming as I tried to unsuccessfully redo my thought processes, but it just was not working. While my head was spinning, the only thing that kept me from pulling the ejection handle again was that Dick Peterson in the back seat would eject with me.

Every part of my being wanted out of that jet. I was 200 miles from home base, over the ocean, and lost in this horrible scenario. I do not know what Dick might have been thinking in the back seat, but I told him to declare an emergency and I turned the flight controls over to him while I fought a fight that I never saw coming.

I looked at the DME indicator, a measurement of distance to home base, and I started watching it and trying to maintain my sanity as each mile passed. I was pounding on the canopy, doing everything I could think of to reorient myself... to no avail. One mile at a time, one breath at a time. I felt my heart was about to explode, but every mile was a victory.

It was the longest half hour of my life, but we finally started our approach to Portland International Airport. Portland was weathered in, and Dick was not trained for the approach and landing, so I took back control of the aircraft.

It was a massive struggle, but I wrestled the F-4 back to the runway, using up half of the runway distance (6,000 feet) just to touch down. Our normal landing target is 1,000 feet on a 12,000-foot runway.

We taxied into a parking spot, shut the engines down and I was frozen. I could not move. The world was still spinning. It took a good while before the crew chief could extricate me from the cockpit. When he did, I could hardly stand up.

So, what happened?

It took months and years to figure it out and accept it. The best flight surgeons in the world, at Brooks Air Force Medical Facility in Dallas Texas, could not really diagnose it. Brooks is the world leader in aviation medicine, and they could not pinpoint the cause. They finally wrote it off to an inner ear infection and put me back on flying status.

"Not so fast," said Colonel Dobler, the group commander, and the one who had hired me. "Your flying days are over. We have lots of pilots vying for this job and we cannot take a chance of putting you back in the air." I fought it and fought it, trying everything to get back into the cockpit of a fighter jet. My passion for flying blinded me to the reality of the situation. In hindsight grounding me made a lot of sense. If I were the commander I would have made the same call.

It was the last flight of my fighter pilot career and the worst situation of my life.

It took weeks to recover my balance and my sanity, but time has a way of healing things.

It turns out that the first psychologist I saw, shortly after the last flight, was right. I did not believe him, and I never went back to see him. I did not want to hear a diagnosis that would end my flying career. He suggested that I had experienced an anxiety attack triggered by a throwback to the fire and ejection from years prior.

Panic attacks are now a part of my life. They are under control most of the time, at least until I get on an airplane. Even as a passenger I need medication to control myself. I remember one international flight to China with Cathy and some dear friends. I forgot to take my pill. Just before takeoff I had an episode where I was fearful for my life and pleaded with the flight attendant to let me off the plane. Fortunately, my good friend Roy Polito was able to talk me down. I medicated myself and calmed down, with no further problems on the flight.

Another scary incident happened in the middle of a dark night while on safari in Africa. I woke up in the middle of the night. I knew I was going to die that night. I woke Cathy and we battled through it. I took a pill, and the medication finally kicked in. For the rest of the safari, I had echos of that terrible night, but I did manage to get in a helicopter and take an air tour of beautiful Victoria Falls a few days later. Everyone insisted that I take the front passenger seat because they knew my fighter pilot history. Little did they know how terrified I was since I had no time to take my chill pill.

I ended up in the Emergency Room on many occasions, including a birthday in Arizona, when I ran myself ragged, tried to drive to the airport, and ended up in the hospital. You guessed it: Panic attack; like my last flight in the F-4 Phantom.

It is hard to write about such a personal subject, and it touches my heart when I hear about celebrities or athletes going public with their own bouts of panic disorder. I was particularly moved when virtual neighbor (Portland, Lake Oswego) and professional basketball all-star, Kevin Love opened up about his struggles. I want you to know, it can happen to fighter pilots as well. But only once. No second chances in that business.

Chapter 27 – Tragedy in the Desert

I remember the wedding. It was Philip and Janet. Cathy and I had flown into Brooklyn, NYC to attend. It was at a funky place called "The Brooklyn Brewery," a craft beer brewery before craft beers came into vogue.

Brother Philip was the 5th child of six in the family, five years my junior. He attended a posh private high school in Buffalo on a needs-based scholarship and everyone there called him "Dutch," and always hassled him about his poverty status.

From there he went on to the Ivy League, graduating from Cornell University. At Cornell, Philip fell in love with the theater and got his degree in Theater Arts. It is a tough career field when you are seeking employment, but he managed, mostly doing technical stuff in the background, and restoring "brownstones" in Manhattan to support his love for the theater.

We were looking forward to their visit to the west coast. They were on a "working vacation," in that they were bringing our stepfather's ashes from Buffalo to Mt Ranier, in Washington State to join our Mom who had passed a couple of years prior. Mom had loved the serenity of Mt. Ranier and insisted that it be her final resting place.

It was about 3 O'clock when I got the call. It was Phil. In a shaken and defeated voice, he said, "We were in a terrible car accident and Janet didn't make it. I am in the hospital, and they are threatening to arrest me."

Within two hours, I was on a flight to Reno, Nevada. The accident occurred in a small town called Elko, three hours out of Reno. After I hit Reno, I stopped to buy a fifth of whiskey before driving to the motel that Phil was staying in at Elko. I figured we both would need it.

As we both nursed a big glass, Philip told me the story. "We were driving in the desert... taking a recreational break from the many hours of highway driving. Janet was driving the Honda. While barreling through the desert Janet hit a culvert (a trench in the desert). The car rolled and Janet wasn't wearing a seatbelt. Her body was thrown partially out the driver's side window, and the car rolled over her, crushing her chest, and killing her instantly."

Philip was stuck now in the desert, with no cell coverage, and in no way prepared for a desert journey. He started to walk in the hot sun, mile after mile, thirsty for water.

There were no main roads in sight and things looked hopeless. Suddenly he saw an old pickup truck in the distance. It was heading his way. He was able to flag down the driver and was rescued.

The Elko police launched an investigation into the crash. They gathered up Janet and towed the totaled Honda into Elko. In the car they found a small stash of pot. At that time Nevada was not the place to be harboring pot. While he was in the hospital tending to his own injuries, the police grilled him mercilessly thinking he might be a drug king pin. "Who is your supplier, etc ,etc." I used all my charm, military rank, and a local attorney to get the cops to back off and let him grieve.

Phil and I drove back to the crash site the next day. He wanted to remember the exact location to be able to go back at a future time to lay flowers.

-     -   -   -   -   -

We are on the picturesque Brooklyn Promenade, with a magnificent view of Manhattan. Cathy and I are excited to bring this part of the story to a happy conclusion. Janet will always be a part of our memory, but time has a way of healing all wounds. Time and Match.com! Philip and Emily met on the dating website and here we are, attending their wedding at this amazing venue.

We are so happy that he found love again, now going on twenty years.

Chapter 28 – They are Trying to Kill Me

It is 2:30 AM and, as a parent, it is a time you do not want the phone to ring. There it goes, waking me from a deep sleep. "Dad I am hiding in the bushes behind Bashes (a grocery store). They are trying to kill me."

I am home in Beaverton, Oregon and Aaron is in Maricopa, Arizona. My wife, Cathy, is in Maricopa as well at our vacation home.

We thought that moving Aaron to Arizona might give him a fresh start. We bought another home in Maricopa at a bargain basement price, and Aaron moved there with his girlfriend. The relationship hit a rough patch, and Aaron was now living on his own.

Back to the phone call: "Hang up and call 911!" I replied," and he did. Emergency vehicles were there in minutes, and they rushed him to the hospital.

Sometimes it seemed that Aaron, who fought so hard to survive as a baby, could not catch a break. He had his front teeth knocked out when a friend accidentally hit him with a golf club. Later he was hit by a car in a parking lot while bike riding and suffered a badly broken leg. That is why he started high school in a wheelchair. Fast forward a few years. He is due to catch a flight from Maricopa, Arizona to his home in Portland, after a quickie surprise Mother's Day trip. As he is slipping on a sock, he lets out a yell. A scorpion had found its way into his sock and stung him. He was in tremendous pain, with a flight to catch in two hours. We did not know what to do. We

placed a call to the poison control center. They said, "Yes,
he will be in a lot of pain, but it is not life threatening."
Off we went to the airport. Aaron made the flight and
had an extremely uncomfortable ride home.

Back to Maricopa:

It is still the middle of the night, and I call Cathy. No
answer. Again, no answer. What to do!!! I called our
next-door neighbor in Maricopa. Tom James is about the
best neighbor you could ask for. He pounds on Cathy's
door and wakes her... and we finally talk. She heads to
the hospital. "It shook me to my inner core," said Cathy,
"How could someone possibly do this to our son? The
tears came down and the prayers went up. I did not know
the severity of his injuries."

Aaron is a mess. His face is badly bruised and swollen
from the beating he took. He had to have eye surgery,

and surgery for a broken cheekbone. A metal plate was inserted, which is still there today.

The story:

Aaron's favorite activity was playing pool at the local pub. This night he had had too many beers to drive home. He called a taxi for a safe ride home and was waiting in front of the bar. He had closed the place down, so it was noticeably quiet. This is how he described the attack: "Out of the shadows a figure appeared and smashed me on the side of the head with an iron bar. I was knocked to the ground and dazed. When I got back up, the stranger was telling me to, 'Get in the car. I have a friend in that truck over there with a gun and laser pointed at your head!' I refused to get in the car and the man started chasing me around it. The man was reaching into his pocket for a knife, and I grabbed his arm, threw him to the ground and started running, finding a hiding place

in the bushes behind the grocery store."

It took Aaron a while to heal physically. It takes even

longer mentally. PTSD rears its ugly head with Aaron on

occasion. I can appreciate that, having had a few bouts

of it myself.

We found out later that some of Aaron's so-called-

friends were in a Mexican drug gang, and he had been

set up. We do not know what their intent was, but it was

potentially a deadly encounter. We expedited Aaron's

departure from Arizona, back to Oregon to get him clear

of his "friends."

Despite his challenges in life, Aaron is one of the most

intelligent and positive people you could meet. Everyone

is Aaron's friend. He has grown into a street smart, savvy

individual that loves life and is always up for a new

adventure. I am proud to call him my son.

Chapter 29 – The Best Decision I Never Made

There are about 30 kids milling about in the park while we wait for the head coach to arrive. It is the first Pee Wee football try out. As an assistant coach I do not have a clue what I am doing, but I put the kids into an old game we played when I was a kid. It is called "last man standing." Thirty young boys (ages 10) stand on one side of the field, and we pick an aggressive young recruit to take the middle of the field. We turn the other twenty-nine loose to run to the other side of the field. The recruit tries to tackle one and then there are two in the middle. It goes on until there are twenty-nine in the middle to tackle the last man standing.

It turns out that the "last man standing" was Jordan, our youngest son. I had no idea he had that kind of talent and aggressiveness. He became the primary running back and linebacker for the Pee Wee team.

He loved football and excelled as a powerful player and all-star right through high school. He dominated both sides of the ball and we spent many Friday nights as proud parents watching him play. He was Captain of the team, head of the Leadership group, and Homecoming King.

His high school coach, Chris Casey, who all the youth and parents loved, sat Jordan down at the end of the season. "Jordan," he said, "You could be an all-star at a Division II college (second tier athletic programs), but you don't have the size to go Division I (top level)." Jordan had his heart set on attending the University of Oregon (Division I).

So, one day Jordan sat down with me and explained his position. "You know how much I love football, and I have made a decision. I have watched my football coaches over the years and most of them have been beaten up and some permanently injured playing football. I have had a great career, but it is not worth the risk of taking it any further. I am done with football!"

I could not have been more proud of him at that moment. For an eighteen-year-old to have that kind of wisdom. Hey, I must have done something right! Way to go Jordan! And he has... onward and upward.

Chapter 30 – When One Door Closes...

It was certainly a brutal way to be cast out of your comfort zone. The only thing that I knew for sure amidst the slow recovery of my mental injuries from "the last flight," was that God had a plan for my life. While I fought and fought to get back into the cockpit of that fighter jet, it just was not going to happen. What commander wants to put a potentially skizzy pilot into one of his fighter jets when there are 25 qualified prospects waiting in the wings. Sad, but true.

The fact is that I had done all I could do in a fighter jet, experienced all the highs one could wish for, and it was time to move on. Fortunately, I had used all of that time in the alert barn, on 48-hour shifts, to better myself, having two Masters degrees, a real estate license and a world of investment knowledge. The only problem... how to put that to use.

It took a while.

The next few years were filled by a cacophony of marginal work in the area of finance, extremely rewarding charitable work, and public speaking.

The effect of my poor Projects upbringing came into play. It was like bondage that held me down, always taking the conservative safe route, and never taking the bold moves that put my education and talent on full display. For years I held back, skimping by instead of moving up, not doing what I knew I had to do to be successful to the full extent of my talent.

I saw a pattern in many of my financial clients. I came to call it "a depression era mentality." They were unwilling to take risks with their money. They could never save enough money, and they could never spend it because there was always that "whatever" lurking in the background.

And then it hit me. I had that very same "depression era mentality." Once I recognized it, I was able to confront it and overcome it... at least that is what I tell myself.

Finally, that bold step! I cast off the meaningless parts of my financial practice to push headlong into a relatively new business, that of fee-based investment management. It took a while, but over the years, I became extraordinarily successful and developed a clientele which was more of a family than a practice.

Miller Financial Group, LLC is an Investment Advisor in Portland, Oregon. I am no longer affiliated with the company, but it is in the able hands of Ben and Todd Newell, a father/son duo and two of my oldest and dearest friends.

I feel very blessed to have experienced such a wide array of experiences in the military, the public domain and in finance. I thank God for that and for the personal rewards he has given me in my beautiful wife and two amazing sons. I look forward to the days ahead as I continue to put my trust in my creator.

ACKNOWLEDGEMENTS

A special thank you to Pierce College Chancellor Emerita Dr Michele Johnson of Tacoma, Washington, for taking the role of chief editor of my book. Her insight, encouragement, inspiration and editing skills provided a depth to my work that I had not anticipated.

The book would not have been possible without an old war veteran and new friend, who was kind enough to share his war experiences through his own book and encouraged me to tell my story. Thanks to Ray Heltsley of Whidbey Island, Washington.

My sister, Valerie Sullivan from McMinnville, Oregon was key in providing important family details and reviewing various aspects of the book.

Emily Winston, sister-in-law from Brooklyn, along with Greg and Rosemary Danford, from Tacoma, Washington were instrumental in providing review and editing for my book.

Ayesha Rasheed, from Pakistan, brought the idea of my cover to life in creating the view I saw from my parachute on that fateful Memorial Day.

Ayesha was an independent contractor provided by a company called Freelancer. I highly recommend Freelancer.com as a source for your future art and publishing needs.

Another belated thank you to Christian Corning, of Sherwood, Oregon, who created the video story of "The Memorial Day Miracle" on the YouTube video platform. (Not to be confused with Sean Elliot sinking the Portland Trailblazers on his amazing shot back in the day). Check it out (not the basketball shot).

And finally, thank you Bree, of "Flourish Photography by Bree," in Tacoma, Washington, for making me look twenty years younger than I am.